ONE NATION,

WISDOM *of*
AMERICAN
Women

ONE NATION,

WISDOM *of* AMERICAN *Women*

THE
POPULAR
GROUP

This book was written by Walnut Grove Press for exclusive use by the Popular Publishing Company.

Popular Publishing Company LLC
1700 Broadway
New York, NY 10019

ISBN 1-59027-068-1

The ideas expressed in this book are not, in all cases, exact quotations, as some have been edited for clarity and brevity. In all cases, the author has attempted to maintain the speaker's original intent. In some cases, material for this book was obtained from secondary sources, primarily print media. While every effort was made to ensure the accuracy of these sources, the accuracy cannot be guaranteed. For additions, deletions, corrections or clarifications in future editions of this text, please write Popular Publishing Company LLC.

Certain elements of this text, including quotations, stories, and selected groupings of Bible verses, have appeared, in part or in whole, in publications produced by Walnut Grove Press of Nashville, TN; these excerpts are used with permission.

Printed in the United States of America
Page Layout Design by Bart Dawson
Cover Design: Tiffany Berry

1 2 3 4 5 6 7 8 9 10 • 02 03 04 05 06 07 08 09 10

Table of Contents

*W*illa Cather wrote, "The history of every country begins in the heart of a man or woman." And so it was with America. The American dream was born in the hearts of both men *and* women, but the history books are chock-full of stories by and about *men*, while the words of notable American *women* are much harder to find. This book is intended to help rectify that situation.

It was not until the 20th century that the women of America truly found their collective voice. Prior to that time, only a few women were able to command the national spotlight. Although the suffrage movement had been active for almost a century, it was not until 1920 that the United States passed the Nineteenth Amendment, giving women the right to vote. In the years since that amendment was passed, the powerful voices of American women have added insight and balance to the national debate.

This text is a collection of wit, wisdom, and all-purpose advice from an assortment of highly quotable American women. On the pages that follow, readers will be reminded of the principles and values that have made, and continue to make, America unique among nations. This collection of quotations tells a story of hope, courage, confidence, and generosity; it conveys a litany of lessons about integrity, adversity, and liberty—all from the perspective of notable women.

Chapter 1

≈

THE PROMISE OF
AMERICA

The future belongs to those
who believe in the beauty
of their dreams.

Eleanor Roosevelt

*T*he American dream is alive and well for men and women alike. Women, of course, have struggled mightily over the last century to gain the rights and opportunities that are now available to all Americans, regardless of gender. Yet, the fight for freedom and equal opportunity is never fully won, so every generation must remain vigilant, and this generation is no different.

Despite its imperfections, America remains the greatest nation on earth: a land of liberty and prosperity. It is a place where dreams can still come true for those who are willing to work hard and smart. It is still the world's great superpower, the world's great economic engine, and the world's great melting pot.

We Americans are blessed beyond measure. Of course, our nation is not without flaws, but it remains a land of opportunity and freedom. And, as grateful citizens, we must do our part to protect America and preserve its liberties just as surely as we work to create better lives for ourselves and our families. On the following pages, noteworthy women remind us that America is a place where dreams still come true . . . for those who are willing to dream courageously *and* work faithfully.

Face a challenge and find joy in the capacity to meet it.

           Ayn Rand

Don't be afraid of the space between your dreams and reality. If you can dream it, you can make it so.

           Bette Davis

When we can't dream any longer, we die.

           Emma Goldman

Too many people put their dreams "on hold." It takes an uncommon amount of guts to put your dreams on the line, to hold them up and say, "How good or bad am I?" That's where the courage comes in.

           Erma Bombeck

One can never consent to creep when one has the impulse to soar.

                    Helen Keller

It is never too late to dream or to start something new.

                    Luci Swindoll

It takes a lot of courage to show your dreams to someone else.

                    Erma Bombeck

If one is lucky, a solitary fantasy can totally transform one million realities.

Maya Angelou

Anyone who fights for the future lives in it today.

Ayn Rand

Everything is in the mind. Knowing what you want is the first step in getting it.

Mae West

I always wanted to be somebody, but I should have been more specific.

Lilly Tomlin

A good goal is like a strenuous exercise—it makes you stretch.

                         Mary Kay Ash

You don't just luck into things; you build step by step, whether it's friendships or opportunities.

                         Barbara Bush

If we are to achieve a richer culture, rich in contrasting values, we must recognize the whole gamut of human potentialities, and so weave a less arbitrary social fabric, one in which each diverse human gift will find a fitting place.

                         Margaret Mead

The young do not know enough to be prudent, and therefore they attempt the impossible and achieve it, generation after generation.

⌐Pearl Buck

There is no chance, no destiny, no fate, that can hinder or control the firm resolve of a determined soul.

⌐Ella Wheeler Wilcox

The idealists and visionaries, foolish enough to throw caution to the winds and express their ardor and faith in some supreme deed, have advanced humanity and have enriched the world.

⌐Emma Goldman

She was a model, a movie actress, and a star on old-time radio. But, it was not until she ventured into the unproven medium of television that Lucille Ball captured the hearts of fans everywhere. Her classic show *I Love Lucy* was number one for just four short years, but it has remained wildly popular for over five decades.

The *I Love Lucy* show began as a dream in the heart of a woman who wanted a career that she could share with her husband, bandleader Desi Arnez. And, the resulting creation has now become a permanent part of the American entertainment landscape.

Lucille Ball had important advice for dreamers of every generation; she observed, "One of the things I learned the hard way was that it doesn't pay to get discouraged. Keeping busy and making optimism a way of life can restore your faith in yourself." So, if you are tempted to abandon *your* dreams, don't. Instead, gather your courage and keep working to make your dreams come true. In America, we can all dream big dreams, and we should . . . just like Lucy.

If you take advantage of everything
America has to offer,
there's nothing you can't accomplish.

Geraldine Ferraro

Chapter 2

THE RIGHTS OF WOMEN

We hold these truths to be
self-evident that all men
and women are created equal.

Elizabeth Cady Stanton

*I*n 1869, the National Woman Suffrage Association was formed in an effort to amend the U.S. Constitution. The organization was led by Susan B. Anthony and Elizabeth Cady Stanton. In the same year, another organization, the American Woman Suffrage Association, was created to lobby state legislatures. This association was led by Lucy Stone.

Several states and territories began granting women the right to vote, beginning with Wyoming in 1869. But, it was not until 1920 that the Nineteenth Amendment to the Constitution created nationwide suffrage for women.

Courageous American women fought unwaveringly for the rights that we enjoy today. May we, too, continue the struggle for liberty and justice, both within our borders and beyond them.

In the new code of laws which it will be necessary for you to make, I desire you would remember the ladies. If particular care and attention are not paid to the ladies, we are determined to foment a rebellion and will not hold ourselves bound by any laws in which we have no voice or representation.

Abigail Adams

Suffrage is the pivotal right.

Susan B. Anthony

The true Republic:
men, their rights, and nothing more;
women, their rights, and nothing less.

Susan B. Anthony

There will never be complete equality until women themselves help make laws and elect law-makers.

᠆᠆*Susan B. Anthony*

I believe that it is as much a right and duty for women to do something with their lives as for men, and we are not going to be satisfied with such frivolous parts as men may give us.

᠆᠆*Louisa May Alcott*

Men of sense in all ages abhor those customs which treat women only as servants.

᠆᠆*Abigail Adams*

Lucy Stone (1818-93) was the first woman to earn a college degree in Massachusetts. Always an independent thinker, she became a leader in both the antislavery and women's suffrage movements. In 1870, she founded *The Women's Journal*, which became the official publication for the American Woman Suffrage Association.

On her deathbed, Lucy Stone spoke to her daughter, Alice Stone Blackwell. Lucy's last words were simple yet profound. She said, "Make the world better." She did, and so should we. Yet, in the busyness and confusion of daily life, the needs of the world may seem distant. We are imperfect human beings struggling to manage our lives as best we can, and we may convince ourselves that we lack the time or the resources to help. When we do so, we do ourselves and our world a profound disservice.

We can never fully repay God for His gifts, but we *can* share them with others. We can never fully repay our ancestors for their sacrifices, but we *can* make sacrifices for the next generation. We can never make this world a perfect place, but we *can* make it a better place. Our country still needs us, and so does the rest of the world. May we act accordingly.

Standing for right when it is unpopular
is a true test of moral character.

Margaret Chase Smith

Chapter 3

❦

PERSONAL GROWTH

I think, somehow, we learn who we really are and live with that decision.

Eleanor Roosevelt

*A*nne Morrow Lindbergh wrote, "Only in growth, reform, and change, paradoxically enough, is true security to be found." Yet, as we encounter the experiences that lead to growth and change, security may seem little more than a distant promise.

It has been said that all of us want to grow but none of us want to change. These words are true, at least in part, for men and women of every generation, but they are especially true for those of this generation. We live in a rapidly changing world, a place where it is difficult to find our bearings and chart our courses. As women, we continue to redefine our roles at home and in the workplace, writing new scripts for our lives as we go.

Embracing change is often difficult, and personal growth is often uncomfortable. Change, of course, is inevitable—growth is not. May we, as mature women, welcome both.

I learned you have to trust yourself, be what you are, and do what you ought to do the way you should do it. You have got to discover yourself, what you do, and trust it.

~Barbra Streisand

The events of our lives happen in a sequence in time, but in their significance to ourselves, they find their own order . . . the continuous thread of revelation.

~Eudora Welty

The delights of self-discovery are always available.

~Gail Sheehy

One of the goals in life is to try to be in touch with one's most personal themes—the values, ideas, styles, colors that are the touchstones of one's individual life, its real texture and substance.

~Gloria Vanderbilt

There's a time in life when we swallow a knowledge of ourselves and it becomes either good or sour inside.

                     Pearl Bailey

I cannot recommend highly enough that people find out who they really are so that they can really experience their lives.

                     Sheryl Crow

I've found that the more I open myself up to messages from the universe, from God, and from my intuition, the more I learn.

                     Gloria Estefan

The greatest challenge of the day is how to bring a revolution of the heart, a revolution which has to start with each one of us.

☙*Dorothy Day*

In the long run, we shape our lives and we shape ourselves. The process never ends until we die.

☙*Eleanor Roosevelt*

As long as one keeps searching, the answers will come.

☙*Joan Baez*

The splendid discontent of God
With chaos, made the world.
And, from the discontent of man
The world's best progress springs.

Ella Wheeler Wilcox

In each of us are places where we have never gone. Only by pressing the limits do you ever find them.

Joyce Brothers

There is no good reason why we should not develop and change until the last day we live.

Karen Horney

The key to change . . . is to let go of fear.

Rosanne Cash

She was born Erma Louise Fiste, but she was far better known by her married name, Erma Bombeck (1927-1996). And, if you're like millions of Americans, you snickered, laughed, and chuckled at her entertaining descriptions of family life. Bombeck wrote from personal experience. It was not until age 37, when her children had reached school age, that she began writing a weekly column for a small Ohio newspaper (she was paid $3.00 per column). Readers loved Erma, and within a few years, her tales of everyday life were carried in 500 newspapers.

Shortly before her death, Bombeck wrote, "When I stand before God at the end of my life, I would hope that I have not a single bit of talent left and could say, 'Lord, I used everything you gave me.'" Hers was a worthy goal, one to which we all should aspire.

We are all blessed with special gifts. We can either use them—or not. We can either continue to grow as individuals—or not. We can either stretch ourselves and, in doing so, risk the temporary sting of failure, or we can avoid risk altogether and suffer the permanent consequences of unfulfilled potential. The words of Erma Bombeck remind us that the time to grow, to risk, and to share is *now*.

Always continue the climb.
It is possible for you to do
whatever you choose, if you first
get to know who you are
and are willing to work
with a power that is greater
than ourselves to do it.

Oprah Winfrey

Chapter 4

COURAGE AND
DETERMINATION

The best protection
any woman can have . . .
is courage.

Elizabeth Cady Stanton

*E*leanor Roosevelt observed, "You gain strength, courage and confidence every time you look fear in the face." But sometimes, when Old Man Trouble rears his head, it's hard to look him squarely in the eye. In fact, when tough times arrive, as they inevitably do from time to time, it is tempting to turn away from Old Man Trouble and run for the hills. But, wise women from every generation understand that the best response to fear is to fight it, not to run from it.

Courage is both contagious and habit-forming. When a woman acts courageously, those around her sense her courage and gain strength from it. And, when she develops the habit of facing her fears sooner rather than later, she creates for herself a life that is characterized by freedom and power rather than by timidity and dread.

It has been said, quite correctly, that courage is its own reward. On the following pages, notable women agree. So, if you need of an extra dose of encouragement to face the inevitable challenges of *your* day, read on. And, as you do, draw strength from the words of women who have talked about courage *and* lived courageously . . . but not necessarily in that order.

Courage is the ladder on which all the other virtues mount.

Clare Booth Luce

It takes courage to lead a life. Any life.

Erica Jong

Do not borrow trouble by dreading tomorrow. It is the dark menace of the future that makes cowards of us all.

Dorothy Dix

I am not afraid of storms, for I am learning how to sail my ship.

Louisa May Alcott

Love is what we were born with. Fear is what we learned here.

Marianne Williamson

A fool without fear is sometimes wiser than an angel with fear.

Nancy Astor

Courage is the price that life exacts for granting peace. The soul that knows it not, knows no release from little things.

Amelia Earhart

Considering how dangerous everything is, nothing is really frightening.

Gertrude Stein

I don't think about risks much. I just do what I want to do. If you gotta' go, you gotta' go.

Lillian Carter

If you're too careful, you are so occupied in being careful that you are sure to stumble over something.

Gertrude Stein

Avoiding danger is no safer in the long run than outright exposure. The fearful are caught as often as the bold.

Helen Keller

My recipe for life is not being afraid of myself.

Eartha Kitt

I never really look for things. I accept whatever God throws my way. Whichever way God turns my feet, I go.

Pearl Bailey

Faith ought not to be a plaything. If we believe, we should believe like giants.

Mary McLeod Bethune

One isn't necessarily born with courage, but one is born with potential. Without courage, we cannot practice any other virtue with consistency. We can't be kind, true, merciful, generous, or honest.

—*Maya Angelou*

I have a lot of things to prove to myself. One is that I can live my life fearlessly.

—*Oprah Winfrey*

What we need is endless courage.

—*Katherine Anne Porter*

Courage, like a muscle, is strengthened by use.

—*Ruth Gordon*

When Mary McLeod Bethune was born in Mayesville, South Carolina, in 1875, few could have guessed that she would change the face of American education. But she did. As a child of former slaves, she picked cotton by day and studied by night. Eventually, she earned a scholarship to Moody Bible Institute in Chicago, where she earned a degree. After teaching school for five years in Georgia and Florida, she founded the Daytona Normal and Industrial Institute for Negro Girls. Today, that school is known as Bethune-Cookman College.

In the beginning, Mary McLeod Bethune operated her school on a shoestring. What was required was faith, and she had more than her share. Bethune once observed, "Without faith nothing is possible. With it, nothing is impossible." And, with little more than her faith and her rugged determination, she built the school from a beginning class of five students to an enrollment of over 1,000. In 1935, Bethune founded the National Council of Negro Women; she was also a trusted advisor to President Franklin Roosevelt.

All of us face adversity, but some face more than others. And, the next time you come face-to-face with the illusion of impossibility, remember Mary Mcleod Bethune, a poor young girl who, against all odds, overcame oppression and changed her world. Then, get busy changing yours.

Become so wrapped up in something
that you forget to be afraid.

Lady Bird Johnson

Chapter 5

&

OBSERVATIONS ON LIFE

You are the only person alive
who has sole custody of your life.

Anna Quindlen

*I*n the 1950's, young Annette Funicello was a glamorous member of television's *Mickey Mouse Club*. And, after the club closed its TV doors in 1959, Annette went on to star in a string of Disney movies. But fame never went to her head. In fact, friends and coworkers were both pleased and amazed that Annette never took herself or her career too seriously. This levelheaded approach to life paid off thirty years *after* she hung up her Mickey Mouse ears when Funicello was diagnosed with multiple sclerosis.

After the shock of her diagnosis had worn off, she approached her disease philosophically, observing simply, "Life does not have to be perfect to be wonderful." Her words remind us that life is, to a surprising extent, a subjective experience that we fashion by the words we speak and the thoughts we think.

Would you like to change certain aspects of your life? Then change your thoughts. Would you like to receive more from your life? Then try putting more into it. Of course, your life will never be perfect, but it *can* be wonderful—and it should be. So assume control and make it so.

Only I can change my life. No one else can do it for me.

Carol Burnett

Life is either always a tightrope or a feather bed. Give me the tightrope.

Edith Wharton

I will not live my life. I will not spend my life. I will invest my life.

Helen Keller

To love what you do and feel that it matters, how could anything be more fun?

Katherine Graham

God has a plan for all of us, but He expects us to do our share of the work.

∽Minnie Pearl

Life isn't a matter of milestones but of moments.

∽Rose Kennedy

Nobody's gonna' live for you.

∽Dolly Parton

Life is a journey… every experience is here to teach you more fully how to be who you really are.

∽Oprah Winfrey

Life loves to be taken by the lapel and told, "I am with you kid. Let's go."

~Maya Angelou

Life is my college. May I graduate well, and earn some honors!

~Louisa May Alcott

You don't get to choose how you're going to die. Or when. You can decide how you're going to live now.

~Joan Baez

An aim in life is the only fortune worth finding.

~Jacqueline Kennedy Onassis

One can never consent to creep when one has the impulse to soar.

&ra;Helen Keller

Do not stop thinking of life as an adventure. You have no security unless you live bravely, excitingly, and imaginatively.

&ra;Eleanor Roosevelt

Working hard and trying to do your best: That's what tennis and life have in common for me.

&ra;Chris Evert

Consider the lilies of the field. Look at the fuzz on a baby's ear. Read in the backyard with the sun on your face. Learn to be happy. And think of life as a terminal illness, because, if you do, you will live it with joy and passion, as it ought to be lived.

Anna Quindlen

The real trick is to stay alive as long as you live.

Ann Landers

Life is a succession of moments. To live each one is to succeed.

Corita Kent

When you cease to make a contribution, you begin to die.

⌖Eleanor Roosevelt

It is up to each of us to contribute something to this sad and wonderful world.

⌖Eve Arden

It is my friends who have made the story of my life.

⌖Helen Keller

All our lives, we are preparing to be something or somebody, even if we don't know it.

Katherine Anne Porter

Whether we're prepared or not, life has a habit of thrusting situations upon us.

Lucille Ball

Life is under no obligation to give us what we expect.

Margaret Mitchell

The more you praise and celebrate your life, the more there is in life to celebrate.

Oprah Winfrey

I don't put limits on my life.

             —Tina Turner

Life hurries past, too strong to stop, too sweet to lose.

             —Willa Cather

I want a busy life, a just mind, and a timely death.

             —Zora Neale Hurston

Life is kicking you in the britches all the time, if you only know it.

             —Katherine Anne Porter

Here, on this side of the grave, here should we labor and love.

Ella Wheeler Wilcox

I learned to love the journey, not the destination. I learned that this is not a dress rehearsal, and that today is the only guarantee you get.

Anna Quindlen

Each day, each moment is so pregnant with eternity that if we "tune in" to it, we can hardly contain the joy.

Gloria Gaither

Mary Cassatt was an American-born artist schooled by the best of the French Impressionists. She has been honored on a U.S. postage stamp; her works are found in the world's finest art galleries; and, she was a noted pupil of the great Edgar Degas. But, her most enduring legacy may be the role she played in introducing French Impressionist art to America.

Cassatt, a woman who made a success of herself in a field that was considered men's work at the time, didn't complain. In fact, she said, "It would be ungracious to grumble." Ungracious, of course, *and* unproductive.

Grumbling about the unfairness of life is, by and large, a waste of precious time and energy. So, if you find yourself regularly attending gripe sessions or pity parties, ask this question: What am I *not* doing to improve my situation? Then, stop complaining and start getting busy changing your world. On the canvas of life, it's never too late to paint a beautiful picture, and the time to pick up the brush is now.

Life is either a daring adventure
or nothing.

Helen Keller

Chapter 6

A FAMILY IS…

Your success as a family
and our success as a society
depend not on what happens
in the White House, but
on what happens inside your house.

Barbara Bush

*Y*our most prized earthly possession is not your home, your car, or your savings account. Your most prized earthly possession is, of course, your family. If you are fortunate enough to be a participating member in a close-knit, loving family, then you are in possession of a priceless bestowal from God. Treasure it, protect it, and nurture it.

Families should be little outposts of security amid the challenges and struggles of daily living. Families should be enclaves of encouragement where all members are not only welcomed, but also valued. Families should be "works in progress," always changing, but never ceasing to love.

Your family is God's gift to you, and it is a gift that must never be taken for granted. So today, take the time to tell a member of your family that you love her or him. And then, do the same thing tomorrow, and the day after that, and the day after that . . . .

The thing I'm the most proud of is my family.

Faith Hill

When you look at your life, the greatest happiness is family happiness.

Joyce Brothers

Having family responsibilities and concerns just has to make you a more understanding person.

Sandra Day O'Connor

I didn't realize what a daddy's girl I was until my daddy was gone.

Dolly Parton

It matters that we should be true to one another, be loyal to what is a family—only a little family in the great Household, but still a family, with family love alive in it and action as a living bond.

‿*Amy Carmichael*

Money can build or buy a house. Add love to that, and you have a home. Add God to that, and you have a temple. You have "a little colony of the kingdom of heaven."

‿*Anne Ortland*

A home is a place where we find direction.

‿*Gigi Graham Tchividjian*

There's a lot to be said for the compassion and understanding that are gained when we've experienced God's grace firsthand as a teenager.

‿*Lisa Whelchel*

I hope that people will say I was there for my family and that I was productive. That's about all I can ask.

⚬*Barbara Eden*

"Suzanne will not be at school today," I once wrote to her teacher. "She stayed at home to play with her mother." I don't remember many other days of her elementary years. But, I remember that day.

⚬*Gloria Gaither*

A house is not a home unless it contains food and fire for the mind as well as for the body.

⚬*Margaret Fuller*

Eden is that old-fashioned house
we dwell in every day
Without suspecting our abode
until we drive away.

Emily Dickinson

Home is where you learn values. It's the responsibility of the family.

Melba Moore

Call it a clan, call it a network, call it a tribe, call it a family. Whatever you call it, whoever you are, you need it.

Jane Howard

What we learn within the family are the most unforgettable lessons that our lives will ever teach us.

Maggie Scarf

Soup is a lot like family. Each ingredient enhances the others; each batch has its own characteristics; and it needs time to simmer to reach the full flavor.

Marge Kennedy

Abigail Adams was married to John Adams for fifty-four years, and, although she had no formal schooling, she taught herself Latin and educated her five children. When son John Quincy Adams was elected, she became the only woman to have been both the wife and the mother of U.S. presidents. Today, of course, Barbara Bush also holds that distinction.

Abigail Adams warned, "We have too many high-sounding words and too few actions that correspond with them." The same can sometimes be said of family life. On occasion, even when we loudly proclaim our love for our families, our deeds don't fulfill the promise of our words.

If you'd like first-rate advice from a special first lady, apply Abigail Adams' formula for success to your own family relations: under-promise and over-serve. It doesn't take a president's wife—or mother—to realize that millions of good intentions pale in comparison to a single good deed. And, as the old saying goes, charity should begin at home . . . *your* home.

The family. We are a strange little
band of characters trudging through life
sharing diseases, toothpaste, coveting
one another's desserts, hiding shampoo,
borrowing money, locking each other
out of rooms, loving, laughing,
defending, and trying to figure out
the common thread that
bound us all together.

Erma Bombeck

Chapter 7

❦

RELATIONSHIPS

Cherish your human connections:
your relationships
with friends and family.

Barbara Bush

So much has been written and said about relationships. In fact, the pursuit of more meaningful relationships has become an American pastime. We can scarcely move through the grocery check-out line without being confronted with dozens of periodicals, all offering "sure-fire" tips for improving our love lives. And, talk show experts offer a near-endless stream of timely tips and sage suggestions for building relationships. If only it were that easy.

Building better relationships is not a matter of reading the right magazine article or discovering the right guru; it is a matter of will. Love takes plenty of time, energy, and commitment. If that sounds like work, it is—but it's worth it.

Do you sincerely seek better relationships? Then begin the hard work of building and maintaining them. And what about all that advice from all those so-called experts? Be forewarned: Their advice never works unless you do.

Love is not leisure; it is work.

Anna Quindlen

The giving of love is an education in itself.

Eleanor Roosevelt

Whoever loves true life, will love true love.

Elizabeth Barrett Browning

Love wins when everything else will fail.

Fanny Jackson Coppin

Love must be learned again and again; there is no end to it. Hate needs no instruction.

◅Katherine Anne Porter

When we come right down to it, the secret to having it all is loving it all.

◅Joyce Brothers

Love is a great beautifier.

◅Louisa May Alcott

Love conquers all except poverty and tooth-aches.

                               Mae West

Nobody has ever measured, not even poets, how much the heart can hold.

                            Zelda Fitzgerald

Love accepts the trying things of life without asking for explanations. It trusts and is at rest.

                           Amy Carmichael

Love doesn't sit there like a stone, it has to be made like bread; remade all the time; made new.

✍*Ursula K. Le Guin*

Love stretches your heart and makes you big inside.

✍*Margaret Walker*

We've grown to be one soul—two parts; our lives are so intertwined that when some passion stirs your heart, I feel the quake in mine.

✍*Gloria Gaither*

Where there is great love
there are always miracles.

Willa Cather

In 1955, the Fulton Theater in New York was renamed in honor of Helen Hayes (1900-1992). Hayes had begun her stage career as a child actress in 1905. Fifty years later, The Helen Hayes Theater became a unique tribute to a unique woman. Miss Hayes once observed, "The story of a love is not important—what is important is that one is capable of love. It is perhaps the only glimpse we are permitted of eternity." She understood that the bonds of love between two human beings are never really broken, not even by death.

Helen Hayes' contemporary Pearl Bailey once quipped, "What the world really needs is more love and less paperwork." Nothing has changed since then; our world still needs less confusion and more love . . . and so do you.

Line by line, moment by moment,
special times are etched into our
memories in the permanent ink
of everlasting love in our relationships.

Gloria Gaither

Chapter 8

KINDNESS AND
GENEROSITY

I must admit that I personally measure success in terms of the contributions an individual makes to her or his fellow human beings.

Margaret Mead

*E*mily Dickinson withdrew from society while in her twenties, but the reclusive young woman was not idle; she wrote poetry. After her death, 1800 poems were discovered, and her works are still widely admired today.

Although Dickinson lived in physical isolation from the outside world, she wrote frequent letters to a select group of close friends. Thus, Dickinson was able to share a message of generosity and hope without leaving the confines of her Amherst, Massachusetts home.

Miss Dickinson wrote, "If I can stop one heart from breaking, I shall not live in vain." Her words still apply. Today, as always, we earn lasting greatness not through acts of self-aggrandizement, but through the small, consistent acts of kindness that, over time, transform the lives of our family and friends.

I am only one, but still I am one; I cannot do everything, but still I can do something; I will not refuse to do the something I can do.

᠆*Helen Keller*

A guest is really good or bad because of the host or hostess who makes being a guest an easy or difficult task.

᠆*Eleanor Roosevelt*

Good manners are nothing more than the practical application of the Golden Rule.

᠆*Loretta Young*

The best time to make friends is before you need them.

⤔Ethel Barrymore

You lose a lot of time hating people.

⤔Marian Anderson

When in need, ask. When in doubt, give.

⤔Marie T. Freeman

Service is the rent you pay
for room on this earth.

Shirley Chisholm

There are two ways of spreading light:
to be the candle, or
to be the mirror that reflects it.

Edith Wharton

You have not lived a perfect day, even though you have earned your money, unless you have done something for someone who will never be able to repay you.

Ruth Smeltzer

An effort made for the happiness of others lifts us above ourselves.

Lydia M. Child

Listening is an art. And the first tenet of the skill is paying undivided attention to the other person.

Mary Kay Ash

Give to the world the best you have and the best will come back to you.

Madeline Bridges

She was the daughter of U.S. Senator Dwight W. Morrow and women's rights advocate Elizabeth Cutter Morrow. She gained fame as the bride of aviator Charles Lindbergh, and she became a best-selling author with her 1955 collection of essays *A Gift from the Sea*. She was Ann Morrow Lindbergh (1906-2001), the woman who observed, "When one is estranged from oneself, then one is estranged from others, too." Her words remind us that in order to establish lasting friendships with others, we must first do so with ourselves.

Do you seek to leave this world a better place than you found it? Then treat everyone with kindness and respect, starting with the woman in the mirror. She deserves it, and so do her friends.

Whenever I meet someone,
I try to imagine her wearing
an invisible sign saying,
"Make me feel important!"
I respond to the sign immediately,
and it works.

Mary Kay Ash

Chapter 9

THE PURSUIT OF HAPPINESS

We carry the seeds of happiness
with us wherever we go.

Martha Washington

*M*artha Dandridge, eldest daughter of John and Frances Dandridge, was born in 1731 on a plantation near Williamsburg, Virginia. At the age of eighteen, she married the wealthy Daniel Park Custis. Two of their babies died, and two others were infants when Custis died in 1757. Two years later, Martha Dandridge Custis married George Washington. After George and Martha had been married for thirty years, George took the oath of office as America's first president, and Martha became America's first First Lady.

Mrs. Washington was known for her understated style and charm. Abigail Adams, who often sat at her right during government functions, described Martha as "one of those unassuming characters who create love and esteem."

Martha Washington understood that genuine happiness always begins on the inside and works its way out from there. She said, "The greater part of our happiness or misery depends on our dispositions, and not on our circumstances." And, what was true in the days of Martha and George is still true today: Happiness depends not upon our acquisitions, but upon our dispositions.

If only we'd stop trying to be happy, we could have a pretty good time.

Edith Wharton

Many persons have the wrong idea about what constitutes true happiness. It is not attained through self-gratification but through fidelity to a worthy cause.

Helen Keller

Joy is what happens to us when we allow ourselves to recognize how good things really are.

Marianne Williamson

This is happiness: to be dissolved in something complete and great.

        Willa Cather

Life really must have joy. It's supposed to be fun!

        Barbara Bush

Laugh and the world laughs with you. Weep and you weep alone.

        Ella Wheeler Wilcox

Make each day useful and cheerful and prove that you know the worth of time by employing it well. Then youth will be happy, old age without regret, and life a beautiful success.

        Louisa May Alcott

I wanted the deepest part of myself to vibrate with that ancient yet familiar longing, that desire for something that would fill and overflow my soul.

Joni Eareckson Tada

Laughter dulls the sharpest pain and flattens out the greatest stress. To share it is to give a gift of health.

Barbara Johnson

Happiness is that state of consciousness which proceeds from the achievement of one's values.

Ayn Rand

Earth's crammed with heaven.

Happiness is not a goal.
It is a by-product.

Eleanor Roosevelt

Learn to value yourself, which means to fight for your happiness.

Ayn Rand

The best and most beautiful things in the world cannot be seen or even touched. They must be felt with the human heart.

Helen Keller

Nothing will kill you quicker than unhappiness.

Phyllis Diller

Each day, look for a kernel of excitement.

Barbara Jordan

Zora Neale Hurston (1891-1960), a graduate of Barnard College, was one of the most prolific writers of the Harlem Renaissance. For a time, she was the most widely read black woman in America, but she was later abandoned by the publishing world. At the time of her death, Hurston was largely forgotten and living on public assistance. She was buried in an unmarked grave. But thankfully, her works were rediscovered, and her books are once again in print.

Hurston observed, "Happiness is nothing but everyday living seen through a veil." And, if you'd like to squeeze a little more enjoyment out of *your* day, don't look far out on the horizon. Your happiness, as Zora Neale Hurston points out, is woven into the very fabric of everyday life. And, if you don't find happiness close to home, you're unlikely to find it anywhere else.

When the dream of our heart
is one that God has planted there,
a strange happiness flows into us.
At that moment, all of the spiritual
resources of the universe
are released to help us.

Catherine Marshall

Chapter 10

PROFESSIONAL
GROWTH

There are no shortcuts
to any place worth going.

Beverly Sills

*B*eing a woman in today's world can be a daunting task. Never have expectations been higher; never have demands been greater; and, never has the workplace been more competitive. But, for women of this generation, the good news is this: never have the opportunities been greater.

The following notable Americans remind us that the journey up the professional ladder is taken one step at a time. Each step requires determination and perseverance, and there can be no guarantees of success. What America offers is the opportunity to climb—through good times and bad—as far up that ladder as your energy and talent can take you.

The world doesn't owe you anything. Nothing is more important than being able to stand on your own two feet.

⁓Lucille Ball

There is no point at which you can say, "Well, I'm successful now. I might as well take a nap."

⁓Carrie Fisher

Whatever I do, I give up my whole self to it.

⁓Edna St. Vincent Millay

Luck is not chance. Fortune's expensive smile is earned.

⁓Emily Dickinson

I have found in work that you only get back what you put into it, but it does come back gift-wrapped.

          Joyce Brothers

Everything works better when you're working.

          Lauren Bacall

Everything worthwhile, everything of any value, has a price. The price is effort.

          Loretta Young

As long as I can work, I'm happy.

          Lucille Ball

God has a plan for all of us, but He expects us to do our share of the work.

Minnie Pearl

Work is life and life is work.

Ruth Gordon

Be decent and fair. But ultimately you have to know how to get the work done, whether or not people like you for it.

Sally Field

Pray as if it's all up to God, work as if it's all up to you.

Anonymous

I long to accomplish a great and noble task, but it is my chief duty to accomplish small tasks as if they were great and noble.

Helen Keller

I seem to have been led, little by little, toward my work; and I believe that the same fact will appear in the life of anyone who will cultivate such powers as God has given him and then go on, bravely, quietly, but persistently, doing such work as comes to his hands.

Fanny Crosby

Ordinary work, which is what most of us do most of the time, is ordained by God every bit as much as is the extraordinary.

Elisabeth Elliot

Don't ever confuse the two, your life and your work . . . The second is only a part of the first.

Anna Quindlen

I don't know anything about luck. I've never banked on it, and I'm afraid of people who do. Luck to me is something else: hard work and realizing what is opportunity and what isn't.

Lucille Ball

The year was 1963, and she was in her mid-forties, a woman searching for a new career. So she took her life savings and started her own business by selling cosmetics the hard way: door to door, one customer at a time. She built the business because of her ability to enlist the enthusiastic support of an energetic sales force. Today that business ranks among the leaders in the cosmetics industry.

Her name? Mary Kay Ash. And she once observed, "A mediocre idea that generates enthusiasm will go farther than a great idea that inspires no one." As you consider *your* professional options, look for a career that excites you, and keep looking until you find it. Then, approach your work with an upbeat attitude and a willing spirit. Finally, the next time opportunity knocks on your door—as it most certainly will—open the door with enthusiasm. After all, excitement is contagious. But, if you want to change the world, the first person you must inspire is yourself.

The secret of joy in work is contained
in one word: excellence.
To know how to do something well
is to enjoy it.

Pearl Buck

Chapter 11

&

OPTIMISM
AND HOPE

Optimism is that faith that leads
to achievement. Nothing can be done
without hope and confidence.

Helen Keller

In 1932, Amelia Earhart became the first woman to fly solo across the Atlantic Ocean. She went on to become a world-traveled public speaker and one of the most notable figures of the first half of the twentieth century. But, she remains best known for what we don't know about her. While attempting to fly around the world in 1937, Amelia Earhart's plane vanished in the South Pacific. No trace was ever found.

Earhart once observed, "Courage is the price life extracts for peace." But, not all of us are wise enough to discover the peace that results from courageous living. Too often, we're held back by silly, irrational fears that cause us to put our lives on hold. Too often, we allow our emotions to be held hostages by pessimism and doubt. Of course, it is never wise to take foolhardy risks, but neither is it wise to let groundless fears rule our lives.

If we are to discover the peace and happiness that life offers each of us, we must face the realities of each day with a spirit of optimism and hope. When we do, fate has a way of smiling upon us. When it does, we, in our wisdom, will smile back.

It was my mother's belief—and mine—to resist any negative thinking.

&~Audrey Meadows

An optimistic mind is a healthy mind.

&~Loretta Young

Far away in the sunshine are my highest inspirations. I may not reach them, but I can look up and see the beauty, believe in them and try to follow where they lead.

&~Louisa May Alcott

If you think you can, you can. And if you think you can't, you're right.

~Mary Kay Ash

Dark as my path may seem to others, I carry a magic light in my heart. Faith, the spiritual strong searchlight, illumines the way, and although sinister doubts lurk in the shadow, I walk unafraid, in the presence of the Lord.

~Helen Keller

Don't bring negatives to my door.

~Maya Angelou

If you can't change your fate, change your attitude.

Amy Tan

Every man is free to rise as far as he's able or willing, but the degree to which he thinks determines the degree to which he'll rise.

Ayn Rand

All that is necessary to break the spell of inertia and frustration is this: Act as if it were impossible to fail. That is the talisman, the formula, the command of right-about-face which turns us from failure towards success.

Dorothea Brande

You must do the thing you think you cannot do.

Eleanor Roosevelt

Keep your face to the sunshine and you cannot see the shadow.

—Helen Keller

A strong positive attitude will create more miracles than any wonder drug.

—Patricia Neal

If you have a negative thought, don't waste hours thinking about it. Simply direct yourself to something positive, and keep repeating the positive until you eliminate the negative.

—Tina Louise

A contempt that drives you through fires and makes you risk everything will make you better than you ever knew you could be.

—Willa Cather

Build a little fence of trust
Around today;
fill each space with loving work
And therein stay.

Mary Frances Butts

She was a preacher's daughter who learned to sing in church. Her professional career spanned six decades, and in 1988 she received a Presidential Medal of Freedom. Her name is Pearl Bailey, and she explained that her success was essentially an exercise in faith. She said, "I never looked for things. I just watched for the way the Good Lord turned my feet, and that's the direction I went."

If you've been guilty of over-planning your life or over-orchestrating the lives of others, perhaps it is time to live on faith, not fear. Perhaps there exists a bigger, better plan for your life, but perhaps you have ignored that plan—or even fought it. If so, it's time to imitate Pearl Bailey and put your feet on a *new* path.

Life is chock-full of synchronicities: open your eyes to them and see where they lead you. Who knows? The world may be hinting at you, tugging at your heartstrings, imploring you to find a new direction. So look carefully for signs and listen carefully to the quiet voice inside. Search not only for a destination, but for a destiny. And, when you find it, follow it with all the strength that you and the Good Lord can muster.

Without faith nothing is possible.
With it, nothing is impossible.

Mary McLeod Bethune

Chapter 12

OVERCOMING
ADVERSITY

It is not in the still calm of life,
or in repose of pacific station
that great characters are formed.
Great necessities call our great virtues.

Abigail Adams

*L*ife is an exercise in personal growth, and the more difficult our circumstances, the more profound are our opportunities to grow. Actress Mary Tyler Moore observed, "It's nice to be successful, but nice isn't the essence of living. Struggle is."

In difficult times, we learn lessons that we could have learned in no other way: We learn about life, but more importantly, we learn about ourselves. Adversity visits everyone—no human being is exempt. It is our duty to learn from the inevitable hardships and heartbreaks of life.

On the pages that follow, notable American women remind us that the struggles of life can help mold us into the people we wish to become. So, if you're facing a difficult situation, be comforted: the struggle is only temporary, but the growth can be permanent.

Face a challenge and find joy in the capacity to meet it.

⌒*Ayn Rand*

If you want the rainbow, you've got to put up with a little rain.

⌒*Dolly Parton*

'Tis easy enough to be pleasant, When life flows along like a song; But the man worthwhile is the one who will smile when everything goes dead wrong.

⌒*Ella Wheeler Wilcox*

The size of your burden is never as important as the way you carry it.

⌒*Lena Horne*

You may encounter many defeats, but you must not be defeated. In fact, it may be necessary to encounter the defeats, so you can know who you are, what you can rise from, how you can still come out of it.

⟿*Maya Angelou*

Birds sing after the storm. Why shouldn't we?

⟿*Rose Kennedy*

There are some things you learn best in calm, and some in storm.

⟿*Willa Cather*

When you come to a roadblock, take a detour.

⟿*Mary Kay Ash*

If you want a place in the sun, you have to expect a few blisters.

—Loretta Young

Although the world is full of suffering, it is also full of overcoming it.

—Helen Keller

To be tested is good. The challenged life may be the best therapist.

—Gail Sheehy

No life is so hard that you can't make it easier by the way you take it.

∽Ellen Glasgow

Flowers grow out of dark moments.

∽Corita Kent

Often God shuts a door in our face so that he can open the door through which he wants us to go.

∽Catherine Marshall

I have always grown from my problems and challenges, from the things that don't work out, that's when I've really learned.

∽Carol Burnett

Everything has its wonders,
even darkness and silence,
and I learn, whatever state I may be in,
therein to be content.

Helen Keller

Nineteenth century doctors called it "brain fever," and Helen Keller was stricken with it at the age of two. When the illness abated, Helen was left deaf and blind. But, with the help of an extraordinary teacher named Anne Sullivan, young Keller learned to communicate, and she quickly embraced education. Eventually, Helen graduated *cum laude* from Radcliffe, and then she went on to become a noted American writer and lecturer.

Keller once observed, "When we do the best we can, we never know what miracles await." That's exactly the kind of red-white-and-blue optimism that has enabled Americans of every generation to overcome adversity. And, if Helen Keller can create her own miracles, so can we.

People are like stained-glass windows.
They sparkle and shine when the sun is
out, but when the darkness sets in,
their true beauty is revealed only
if there is a light from within.

Elizabeth Kübler-Ross

Chapter 13

❧

SELF-
ACCEPTANCE

Look for the good in everybody,
starting with yourself.

Marie T. Freeman

*E*lla Wheeler Wilcox was no stranger to the pen. Initially applying her talents to journalism, Wilcox (1855-1919) wrote a daily poem for a syndicate of newspapers. Later, over twenty volumes of her verse were published. In her poem "Optimism," she had this advice: "Say that you are well and all is well with you, and God will hear your words and make them true."

The self-fulfilling prophecy is alive and well, and hard at work. If we constantly anticipate the worst, the worst is what we will attract. And, if we constantly berate ourselves, we will create negative stereotypes that do us great harm. But, if we think positive thoughts about ourselves and our world, then we put the self-fulfilling prophecy to work in the service of our own best interests.

Do you seek to improve some important aspect of your life? Start by accepting the person you are today. Then, visualize the person you want to become tomorrow. When you do, God will hear your thoughts and make them true.

No one can make you feel inferior without your consent.

Eleanor Roosevelt

The most freeing thing is to like your imperfections.

Mary Tyler Moore

Everybody must learn this lesson somewhere— it costs something to be what you are.

Shirley Abbott

It took me a long time not to judge myself through someone else's eyes.

∾*Sally Field*

Always be a first-rate version of yourself instead of a second-rate version of someone else.

∾*Judy Garland*

You cannot belong to anyone else until you belong to yourself.

∾*Pearl Bailey*

Learn to value yourself, which means to fight for your happiness.

∾*Ayn Rand*

Being a star means that you find your own special place and shine right where you are.

Dolly Parton

Never bend your head. Always hold it high. Look the world straight in the eye.

Helen Keller

It is best to act with confidence, no matter how little right you have to it.

Lillian Hellman

Follow your instincts. That is where true wisdom manifests itself.

Oprah Winfrey

Trust your instincts. And never hope more than you work.

Rita Mae Brown

It doesn't do any good to put yourself down. If other people are going to have negative thoughts, that's their problem.

Carol Burnett

No one can figure out your worth
but you.

Pearl Bailey

At an age when most people have long settled into retirement, this spry septuagenarian embarked on a career that won worldwide recognition. At the age of seventy-six, and without the benefit of a single art lesson, Grandma Moses took up painting. Having been a busy housewife throughout adulthood, she had embroidered wool pictures on canvas as a hobby. But, when her fingers became too stiff to handle a needle, Grandma didn't quit— she just began painting. Her colorful country scenes now hang in museums all over the world.

Grandma Moses (1860-1961) once said, "Life is what we make it. Always has been. Always will be." One way that you can make *your* life better is to learn the art of self-acceptance. If your sternest critic resides between your two ears, fire that critic and hire a cheerleader. If you still berate yourself for past indiscretions, forgive yourself and move on. Life is far too short to spend it on chronic fault-finding, *especially* if the faults you chronically find are your own.

There ain't nothing from the outside
can lick any of us.

Margaret Mitchell

Chapter 14

ALL-PURPOSE
ADVICE

Advice is what we ask for
when we already know the answer,
but wish we didn't.

Erica Jong

We Americans are the great givers of advice. We freely offer our recommendations, suggestions, tips, hints, insights, opinions, communications, instructions, warnings, appeals to better judgement, bright ideas, and words to the wise. From the self-help section of the local bookstore to the Dear Abby column in the local newspaper, we Americans gobble up advice and then keep gobbling. Hopefully, most of this advice has two overriding characteristics: first, that it is helpful, and second, that it is acted upon. With that thought in mind, we conclude with an abbreviated assortment of admonitions from an assemblage of astute American women. Read and heed.

A life of reaction is a life of slavery, intellectually and spiritually. One must fight for a life of action not reaction.

Rita Mae Brown

Fill what's empty. Empty what's full. Scratch where it itches.

Alice Roosevelt Longfellow

Take the back roads instead of the highways.

Minnie Pearl

We turn not older with years, but newer every day.

Emily Dickinson

If you listen to your conscience,
it will serve you as no other friend
you'll ever know.

Loretta Young

The worth of every conviction consists precisely in the steadfastness with which it is held.

~Jane Addams

Today is a new day. You will get out of it just what you put into it.

~Mary Pickford

Character building begins in infancy and ends in death.

~Eleanor Roosevelt

Common sense is the knack of seeing things as they are, and doing things as they ought to be done.

~Harriet Beecher Stowe

The most exhausting thing in life, I have discovered, is being insincere. That is why so much social life is exhausting; one is wearing a mask.

⟜*Anne Morrow Lindbergh*

I pray, but I don't pray to win. I pray for the inspiration to give my best.

⟜*Althea Gibson*

If we could sell our experiences for what they cost us, we would all be millionaires.

⟜*Abigail Van Buren*

Some New Year's Resolutions: I'm going to clean this dump just as soon as the kids grow up. I will go to no doctor whose plants have died. I'm going to apply for a hardship scholarship to Weight Watcher's. I will never loan my car to anyone I have given birth to. And, just like last year, I am going to remember that my children need love the most when they deserve it the least.

⟜*Erma Bombeck*

I do not believe in failure. It is not failure if you enjoyed the process.

Oprah Winfrey

Don't be afraid to fail. Even if you do, you're bound to learn something along the way.

The Delaney Sisters

There are no hopeless situations; there are only people who have grown hopeless.

Clare Boothe Luce

I pray hard, work hard, and leave the rest to God.

Florence Griffith Joyner

Trust your hunches.... They are usually based on facts filed away below the conscious. But be warned: Don't confuse hunches with wishful thinking.

Joyce Brothers

There are no mistakes, no coincidences; all events are blessings given to us to learn from.

Elizabeth Kübler-Ross

The days in my life that stand out most vividly are the days I've learned something. Learning is so exciting that I get goose bumps.

Lucille Ball

To get it right, be born with luck or else make it. Never give up. Get the knack of getting people to help you and also pitch in yourself.

Ruth Gordon

Heat is required to forge anything. Every great accomplishment is the story of a flaming heart.

Mary Lou Retton

When you get into a tight place and every-thing goes against you, till it seems as though you could not hang on a minute longer, never give up then, for that is just the place and the time the tide will turn.

Harriet Beecher Stowe

Love the moment and the energy of the moment will spread beyond all boundaries.

Corita Kent

You are unique, and, if that is not fulfilled, some-thing has been lost.

Martha Graham

Bromidic though it may sound, some questions don't have answers, which is a terribly difficult lesson to learn.

          Katherine Graham

Never be afraid to sit awhile and think.

          Lorraine Hansberry

Acceptance says, "True, this is my situation at the moment. I'll look unblinkingly at the reality of it. But I'll also open my hands to accept willingly whatever a loving Father sends me."

          Catherine Marshall

The greatest challenge of the day is how to bring a revolution of the heart, a revolution which has to start with each one of us.

          Dorothy Day

A complete holiday from self-pity is necessary to success.

                                   Dorothea Brand

I feel there are two people inside me: me and my intuition. If I go against her, she'll defeat me every time, and if I follow her, we get along quite nicely.

                                   Kim Basinger

Simplify everything you do right down to the bare essentials.

Billie Jean King

People say, "What is the sense of our small effort?" They cannot see that we must lay one brick at a time, take one step at a time.

Dorothy Day

Certain springs are tapped only when we are alone.

Anne Morrow Lindbergh

Imagine what you want to do, not what you don't want to do.

Sandra Haynie

My mother drew a distinction between achievement and success. She said that achievement is the knowledge that you have studied and worked hard and done the best that is in you. Success is being praised by others. That is nice but not as important or satisfying. Always aim for achievement and forget about success.

Helen Hayes

Be different, stand out, and work your butt off.

Reba McEntire

You have to love a nation that celebrates its independence every July 4th, not with a parade of guns, tanks, and soldiers who file by the White House in a show of strength and muscle, but with family picnics where kids throw Frisbees, the potato salad gets iffy, and the flies die from happiness. You may think you have overeaten, but it is patriotism.

Erma Bombeck